little book BIG

What is science?

NoodleJUICE

Noodle Juice Ltd
www.noodle-juice.com
Stonesfield House, Stanwell Lane, Great Bourton, Oxfordshire, OX17 1QS
First published in Great Britain 2023
Copyright © Noodle Juice Ltd 2023
Text by Noodle Juice 2023 • Illustrations by Katie Rewse 2023
All rights reserved
Printed in China
A CIP catalogue record of this book is available from the British Library.
ISBN: 978-1-915613-71-4
1 3 5 7 9 10 8 6 4 2

FSC
www.fsc.org
MIX
Paper | Supporting responsible forestry
FSC® C005748

This book is made from FSC®-certified paper. By choosing this book, you help to take care of the world's forests.
Learn more: www.fsc.org

What is science?

Science is the way we learn about the natural world by observing and experimenting. Science helps us to explain how the world works.

Let's ask some questions to see if we can work out what science means to us!

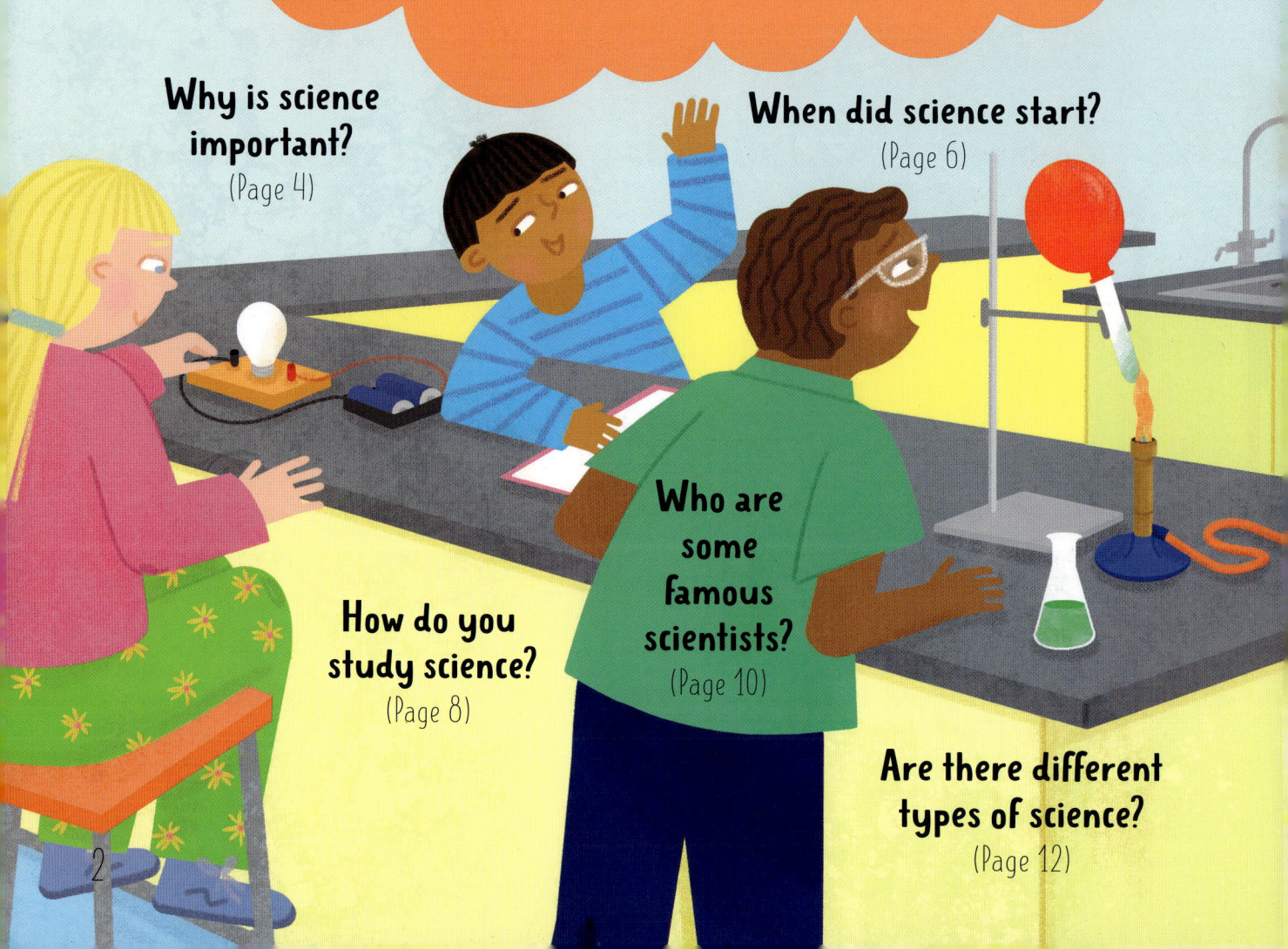

Why is science important?
(Page 4)

When did science start?
(Page 6)

How do you study science?
(Page 8)

Who are some famous scientists?
(Page 10)

Are there different types of science?
(Page 12)

What is physics?
(Page 14)

What is chemistry?
(Page 16)

What is biology?
(Page 18)

What are earth sciences?
(Page 20)

$$NaHCO_3(s) + HC_2H_3O_2(aq)$$
$$\rightarrow NaC_2H_3O_2(aq)$$
$$+$$
$$H_2O(l) + CO_2(g)$$

What can you do with science?
(Page 22)

What is the future of science?
(Page 24)

Is science always good?
(Page 26)

3

Why is science important?

Science is important because it helps us find solutions to problems. Science helps to explain where we came from and how we can improve things for the future. It helps us to understand how and why things function.

Science helps us develop new **technologies** to improve our lives.

It allows us to **explore** different ways of thinking.

Studying science can help us make better **decisions**.

Science teaches us to be **curious**.

5

When did science start?

People observed the stars and seasons as long ago as 2500 BCE. It wasn't until 600 BCE that the first natural philosophers – or early scientists – tried to explain how the universe works.

Ancient Greek philosophers studied the natural world and looked at elements such as water. One philosopher, Thales, invented the study of geometry.

But not all of them agreed with one another. This led to another key part of science – the ability to be CRITICAL of someone else's arguments and to challenge their thinking.

Pythagoras (c.570 BCE–c.490 BCE) believed that **numbers** were very important in science.

Aristotle (384 BCE–322 BCE) made **sense** of the world around him by asking what an object's purpose was.

Archimedes (c.287 BCE–212 BCE) studied maths and is famous for his work on **levers**.

Hippocrates invented the science of **medicine** in the 5th century BCE.

* CE stands for Common Era which started at the year 0000. BCE stands for Before Common Era. This book was published in 2024 CE.

How do you study science?

A scientist studies something by observing it and recording the information they discover. Let's consider water. What might a scientist want to know about it?

How much does it **weigh**?

Does it **change** form at different temperatures?

Does it have a **smell**?

What does it **look** like?

What does it **feel** like?

A scientist then might create a hypothesis. Say it like this:

HI-po-thuh-SIS

A hypothesis is a theory or idea about something that a scientist tries to prove or disprove.

We know that when you heat water some of it turns to steam and **evaporates**. A hypothesis could be: if you boil 100ml water for one minute, half of it will disappear.

Scientists can conduct an **experiment** to find out if this happens.

Who are some famous scientists?

Zhang Heng (79-139) was the first astronomer to map the stars and planets.

Ibn al-Haytham (965-1040) was an early mathematician who studied how we see light.

Nicolaus Copernicus (1473-1543) first suggested that the sun was the centre of our universe.

Isaac Newton (1642-1727) is famous for his work on gravity.

Carl Linnaeus (1707-1778) studied plants and invented a way to classify living things.

Mary Anning (1799-1847) is famous for finding fossils from the Jurassic period.

Charles Darwin (1809-1882) studied how animals can change to form new species.

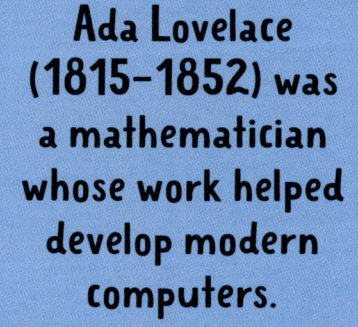

Ada Lovelace (1815-1852) was a mathematician whose work helped develop modern computers.

Alexander Graham Bell (1847-1922) patented or registered the first telephone.

Marie Curie (1867-1934) discovered two new radioactive elements.

Albert Einstein (1879-1955) is famous for his theory of relativity which deals with gravity and movement.

Alan Turing (1912-1954) was a computer scientist who cracked the German naval Enigma code during World War II.

$E = mc^2$

Francis Crick (1916-2004) and James Watson (1928-) discovered the structure of DNA, the building blocks of the human body.

Jane Goodall (1934-) studied chimpanzees to help us better understand human behaviour.

Stephen Hawking (1942-2018) is an expert on black holes and the universe.

Tim Berners Lee (1955-) invented the world wide web.

Are there different types of science?

There are probably as many different types of science as there are things you can think of. Here are just a few subjects scientists choose to study.

Food

Movement

Living things

Space

The human body

Light

The Earth

Forces

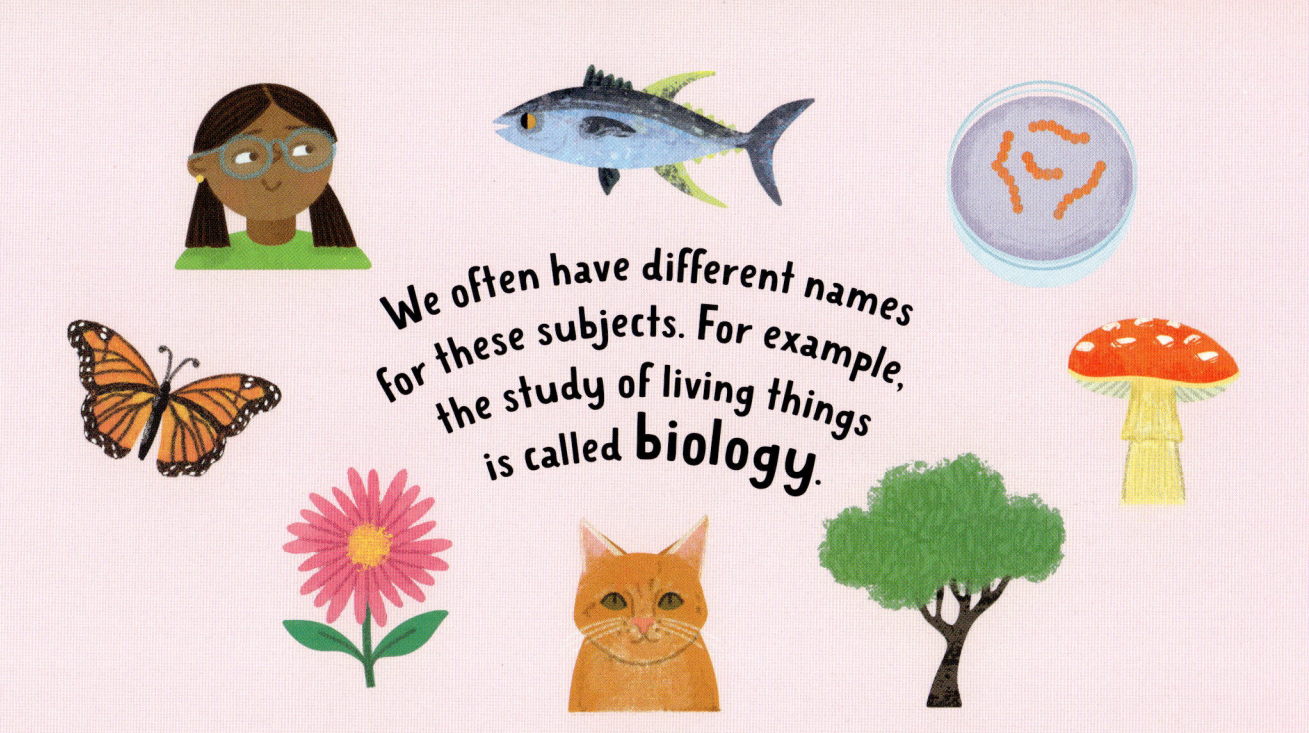

We often have different names for these subjects. For example, the study of living things is called **biology**.

A scientist who studies space is called an astrophysicist. Say it like this:

ASS-TROH-FIZZ-ih-CIST

They investigate the origin and structure of the universe, including its stars, galaxies, planets and black holes.

What is physics?

Physics is the study of matter and energy. Matter is anything that has weight and takes up space. Energy is strength and power and enables things to work.

People who study physics are called physicists.

Matter comes in three main forms:

Solid

Liquid

Gas

Energy has a few more:

Radiant, or light

Renewable

Kinetic, or movement

Electric

Potential, or stored

Thermal, or heat

By studying matter and energy, physicists hope to find a set of rules that govern every part of our universe, from the very small to the very large.

What is chemistry?

Chemistry is the study of the elements, such as oxygen or gold, that make up the universe. Chemists investigate what elements do and how they react with other elements in order to make new ones.

There are 118 different elements in the universe that we know about.

They are grouped together in what is called the **Periodic Table**. Each element has a different symbol to represent its name.

Each element is made up of atoms. An **atom** is the smallest particle of that element.

An atom is made from **protons**, electrons and neutrons.

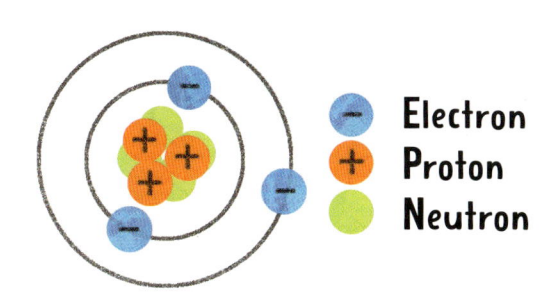

- Electron
+ Proton
- Neutron

The simplest element is **hydrogen**. It has one proton and one electron in each atom. Hydrogen is a gas.

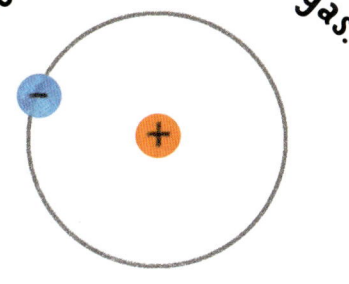

But if you add **two** atoms of hydrogen (H) to **one** atom of oxygen (O) (also a gas), you will create **water** (H_2O).

Chemists study how elements interact and help to explain how things around us happen. They use their knowledge to create new materials to benefit us and our planet.

What is biology?

Biology is the study of living things. A biologist will examine how an organism behaves, what it looks like, how it survives, where it lives and how it moves.

Animals, including humans, can be split into different groups depending on certain characteristics.

Mammals

Birds

Reptiles

In the 1750s, Swedish scientist **Carl Linnaeus** developed a system of classification that we still use today.

There are **three** main subjects you can choose to study as a biologist.

Botany is the study of plants. Say it like this:

Boh-TAN-ee

Zoology is the study of animals. Say it like this:

Zoo-OL-oh-gee

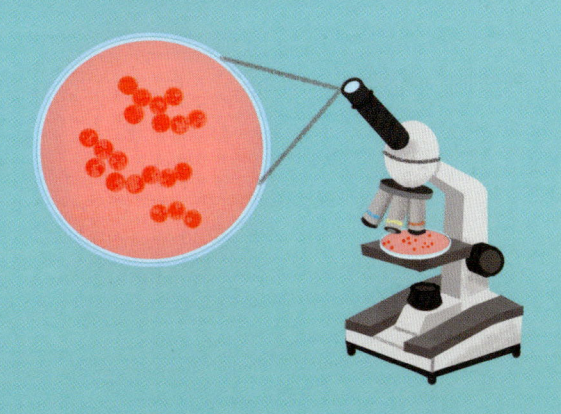

Microbiology is the study of microorganisms or very tiny creatures which you can't see with the human eye. Say it like this:

My-CRO-by-OL-oh-gee

What are earth sciences?

Scientists who study earth sciences can be called geologists. They look at how the Earth was created and what makes up our planet, as well as the moon and other planets such as Mars.

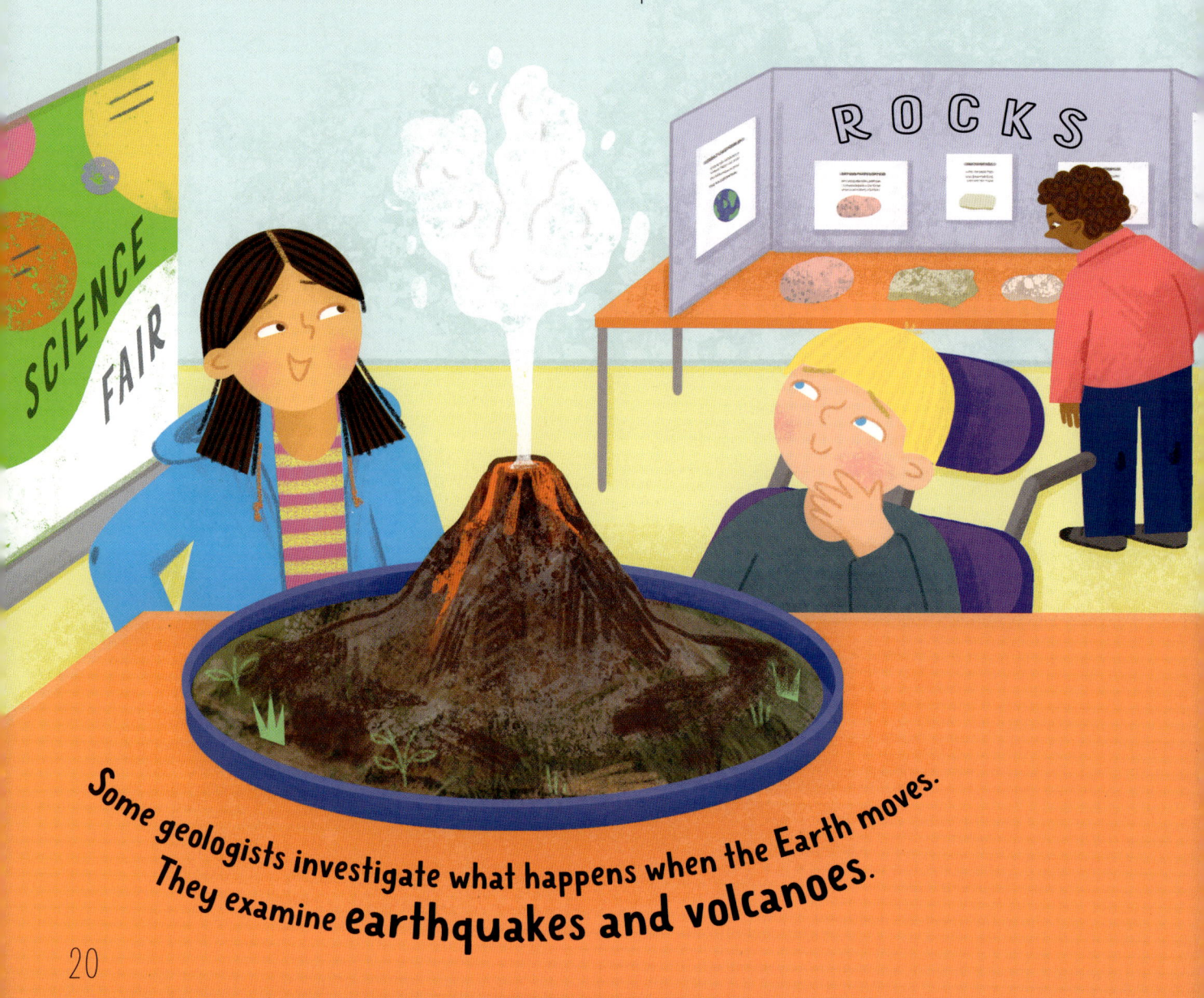

Some geologists investigate what happens when the Earth moves. They examine **earthquakes and volcanoes**.

Others study the soil in which we grow our food. They help to improve the **quality** of the soil which means we can grow better and tastier crops.

Some geologists focus on **rocks** and minerals.

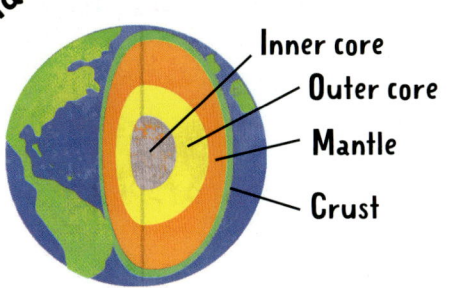

They investigate the structure of the **planet**, both its surface and its interior.

- Inner core
- Outer core
- Mantle
- Crust

People who study earth sciences help us to make the best use of the resources our planet has to offer, as well as helping protect the environment for the future.

What can you do with science?

There are lots of things you can do if you are interested in science.

You could become a teacher and inspire children to learn more about it.

You could find new ways to reduce the use of fossil fuels.

And help people to understand how we can save the planet.

You could discover a new treatment to **cure** illness.

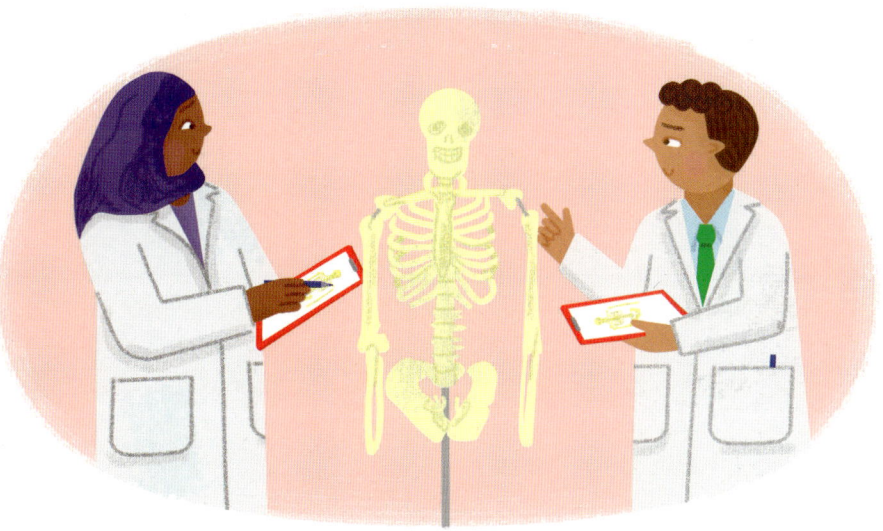

You could invent a solution to **single use plastic**.

You could even invent **teleporter** technology.

What else do you think you could do with science?

What is the future of science?

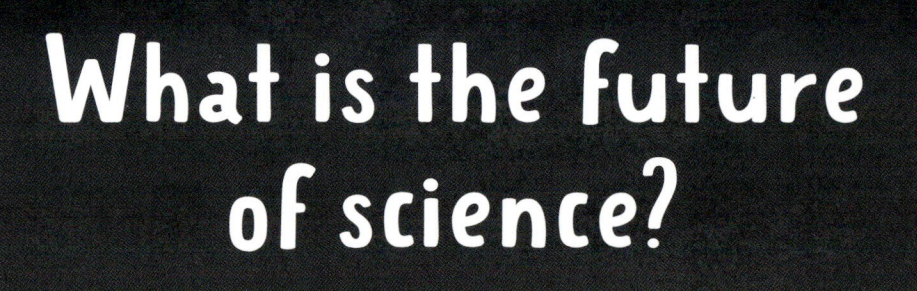

Scientists discover new things every day. What was once thought to be magic, such as electric lighting, is now common in most homes on the planet.

Here are some of the scientific possibilities that lie ahead:

Scientists could create **human organs** from scratch using DNA manipulation.

Truly artificially **intelligent** computers,

We may be able to easily travel through space and **populate** other planets.

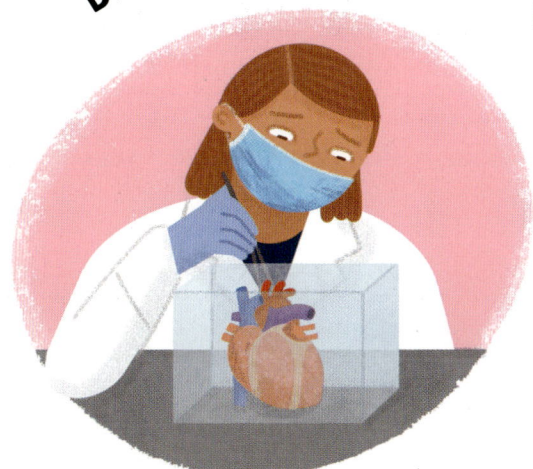

Instead of typing our messages, we may be able to simply **think** of them and have our words appear on screen.

We could choose to **extend** how long we live for.

But it's more important how we answer the questions that science raises.

25

Is science always good?

Science has helped people improve their lives since the 16th century. With every advance in scientific knowledge, more ideas and inventions appear that make our lives easier.

But sometimes an invention that can **benefit** humanity...

...can also cause us **harm**.

Science, in itself, is neither good nor bad. What is important is how we choose to use that science.

So ... do we know what science is?

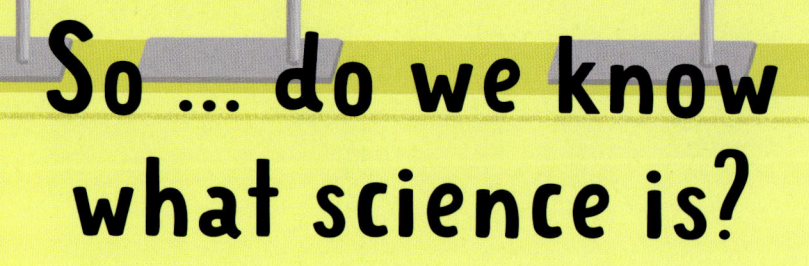

We know that science is important as it teaches us how things work.

We know WHEN science started.

We understand HOW we study science.

We know the different TYPES of science.

We know WHO studies science.

We know how USEFUL science can be and how it can help us.

We know that SCIENCE is really important when thinking about our future.

But science and technology is developing quickly. We need to understand what we CAN do with science and what we SHOULD do. Science isn't good or bad, but our decisions can be.

Why don't you think about which area of science you would like to explore further?

Glossary

Advance	to move forward	**Decision**	a conclusion reached after some consideration
Astronomer	someone who studies space and the objects in it	**Evaporate**	turn from liquid into gas
Black hole	a region of space where matter has collapsed in on itself	**Experiment**	a scientific process followed to make a discovery, demonstrate a known fact or test a hypothesis
Challenge	a call to prove or justify something	**Extend**	to make larger or longer
Characteristic	typical of a person, animal, place or thing	**Fossil fuel**	a natural fuel, such as coal or gas, made in the past from living organisms who have died
Classify	to group or arrange things according to shared categories	**Function**	work or operate in the proper or normal way
Common	shared by, coming from, or done by two or more things	**Galaxy**	a system of millions or billions of stars, with gas and dust, held together by gravity
Consider	to think carefully about something	**Geometry**	a branch of maths that studies points, lines, surfaces and solids
Critical thinking	the objective analysis of an issue to form a judgement	**Govern**	to exert a guiding influence in or over
Curious	eager to know or learn about something		

Gravity	the force that attracts a body towards the centre with a large mass	**Populate**	cause people to settle in a place
Interact	to have an effect on each other	**Purpose**	the reason why something exists
Interior	the inside of something	**Radioactive**	an element that gives off radiation without an external cause
Mathematician	an expert in maths	**Solution**	a way to solve a problem
Natural world	all the animals, plants and other things that exist in nature and are not made by people	**Surface**	the uppermost layer of something
		Technology	the branch of knowledge dealing with engineering and science
Naval	to do with the navy	**Teleporter**	an imaginary form of very fast transport
Observe	to notice or mark something	**Universe**	all existing matter and space
Organism	an animal, a plant or a single-celled life form		
Origin	the point or place where something begins		
Philosopher	a person who offers opinions on important questions in ethics, logic and human thought